KING AR...UR
IN THE WEST

Felicity Young
and
Michael Williams

BOSSINEY BOOKS

First published in 1993 by Bossiney Books, St Teath, Bodmin, Cornwall.

Typeset and printed by Penwell Ltd, Callington, Cornwall.

© Felicity Young and Michael Williams

ISBN 0948158 83 2

ACKNOWLEDGEMENTS
Front cover photography: ROY WESTLAKE
Front cover design: MAGGIE GINGER
Back cover photography: MICHAEL and ROSEMARY CLINCH
Other photographs: RAY BISHOP; MICHAEL DEERING;
                   BARRY ENGLEFIELD; ROY WESTLAKE
Drawings: FELICITY YOUNG

ABOUT THE AUTHOR

MICHAEL Williams, a Cornishman, started full-time publishing in 1975. He and his wife Sonia live in a cottage on the shoulder of a green valley just outside St Teath in North Cornwall.

In addition to writing and publishing, Michael Williams is a keen cricketer and collector of cricket books and autographs. He was the first captain of the Cornish Crusaders Cricket Club and is today President of the Crusaders.

Michael and Sonia Williams lived for ten years at Bossiney near Tintagel, in that time his interest in the subject of Arthur deepened and broadened. His earlier works include a guide to Tintagel; he is co-author of King Arthur in Cornwall *and* King Arthur in Somerset *and he has made several radio broadcasts on Arthur and related subjects.*

As a publisher he now operates in six regions: Cornwall, Devon, Dorset, Somerset, Avon and Wiltshire.

KING ARTHUR IN THE WEST

K ING ARTHUR is a fascinating historical story. For hundreds of years people have been telling Arthur stories, but they are more profound than just good yarns. Only a powerful theme, only something answering to some deep sense of British character – and need – would have been sustained for so long.

When we think of Arthur, we do not think of just one character. In our mind's eye we see a whole theatre of people and places, themes and ideals. We can almost hear the clash of sword in battle. There alongside the King is Guinevere, his Queen, and his wise man Merlin. We see Camelot: royal mysterious Camelot. We see too Lancelot, pledged to noble aims but ... there is the round table, the magical sword Excalibur and a great deal more. The ifs and buts: the impossibility of it all, and yet the probability.

More than eight centuries ago a Welsh monk, residing in Oxford, wrote the first bestseller in the history of British publishing.

The author was Geoffrey of Monmouth, and his handwritten book was *History of the Kings of Britain*. Colin Wilson, writing in the *Western Morning News* in October 1992, referred to it as: 'that extraordinary ragbag of legends, rumours and downright lies.'

That may be so but only after Geoffrey of Monmouth – and indeed because of him – did the Arthurian theme really come to life. The writing of the Welshman enabled succeeding writers to develop and expand.

We in Cornwall naturally think Geoffrey chose wisely in selecting Tintagel as the birthplace of Arthur. A dramatic fortress on a wild stretch of coastline, it is a place to fire the imagination.

ARTHUR AS a babe being handed to Merlin from the postern gate of Tintagel Castle. This oil painting, by the Victorian artist W.H. Hatherell RI, is part of an impressive display of Arthurian art at King Arthur's Great Halls at Tintagel, North Cornwall.

Cornwall has so many Arthur place names – or locations with a related Arthurian story – that we feel bound to ask the question: 'Can there be smoke without fire?'

There is a story which we like to think is true. It dates back to the thirteenth century when a certain abbot was speaking to a congregation of monks. Many of his congregation had fallen asleep; some were even snoring.

In desperation, the abbot raised his voice and declared: 'I will tell you something new and great. There was once a mighty king, whose name was Arthur ...'

Those eighteen words had an electrifying effect. His congregation, who could not stay awake to hear his wise thoughts on holy matters, were agog at the mention of that magical name: Arthur.

Here in Cornwall we know something about the strength of feeling on matters concerning Arthur. In 1146 some canons of Laon Cathedral were in Cornwall on a fund-raising mission. They came to Bodmin. They brought with them an image of Our Lady which they believed had the ability to heal the sick. A man with a withered arm came hoping to be healed. 'Just as the Bretons are wont to wrangle with the French on behalf of King Arthur, the man began to dispute with one of our company, saying Arthur was still living.' A furore erupted, 'it came to bloodshed' and no cure could be performed.

In Cornwall we therefore understand there is often no grey area in many an Arthurian debate. The blood and broken bones of that market place in Bodmin are vivid reminders of that fact.

Anyone embarking on this Arthurian expedition quickly encounters a second question, even puzzle. There is this fascinating blend of history and legend, so entwined that we feel compelled to ask 'Where does history end and legend begin?' And, of course, the different versions and the different theories add to the complexity.

Inevitably, too, in a publication of this size it has been necessary to compress. To do justice to the whole Arthur scene in the West would require a thousand pages.

These Arthurian stories and locations are scattered all over the Westcountry – though principally in Somerset and Cornwall where we begin. They are a marvellous invitation to explore these

A SMALL DREAMER absorbs the magical atmosphere of Tintagel, the sunlight glinting on the sea and the cliffs rising starkly above her. The time of Arthur and his knights seems close at such moments.

ancient landscapes.

In visiting them we have experienced a thrill of discovery – and found in and around them an energising quality.

THE KNIGHTING of Galahad by Sir Lancelot, by William Hatherell RI, at King Arthur's Great Halls, Tintagel.

THE GRAIL TRADITION

JOHN MATTHEWS in his thoughtful, thought-provoking *The Elements of The Grail Tradition*, first published in Britain by Element Books Ltd of Longmead, Shaftesbury, Dorset in 1990, said: *'The Grail Tradition is the embodiment of a dream, an idea of such universal application that it appears in a hundred different places as the teaching of sects, societies and individuals. Yet, although its history, both inner and outer, can for the most part be traced, it remains elusive, a spark of light glimpsed at the end of a tunnel, or a reflection half-seen in a swiftly-passed mirror.'*

Curiously enough the original meaning of this word 'Grail' was not 'holy' in the accepted Christian style. Long before the stable birth of Christ at Bethlehem, the concept of the Grail existed. The Grail, like numerous other pagan ideas, was absorbed by the Christian Church in its early days. It became a symbol of ideal, of purity and quality of character – especially after it had become part of the Arthurian cycle of legends. Of the Knights of the Round Table, only the spiritual, somewhat unworldly Percival was successful in his quest.

The legends of the Holy Grail, like Stonehenge, are wrapped in mystery. They retain a secret seemingly beyond our grasp.

Two things, though, stand out like Brown Willy and Rough Tor on Bodmin Moor on a diamond-sharp day. First Arthur is essentially about a search – our search – and secondly, at the very soul of the whole business, is an endeavour by us to find our best self – or selves.

THE BIRTH OF ARTHUR

'*A*LL LIFE BEGAN *in water; this land was once under water, the story of Arthur, the hero of its longest-lived and most potent legend, is seen against water. He was said to have been conceived at Tintagel, therefore in the sound of terrific seas; to have reclaimed Britain from its barbarian invaders in twelve great battles, five of which were fought on the shores of rivers; to have been mortally wounded during civil war in a battle fought, again, on a river; to have resigned his sword Excalibur to a water spirit, whose arm rose out of a lake to take it back, and to have been borne away across water, dying but never to die.*'

That is how Elizabeth Jenkins opened her brilliant *The Mystery of King Arthur*, published by Michael Joseph back in 1975.

So it is to Tintagel that we come for the birth of Arthur. Here the roar of the Atlantic can be as loud as the wind on a stormy day. In fact Sir John Betjeman, who loved and understood the changing mood and moods of North Cornwall, once reflected 'This slaty sea coast parish is best seen out of season and on a stormy day.' Sir John may be right, but we both know the glory of the sun sinking into the face of the ocean 'from something like a flaming battlefield.' At Tintagel the line dividing fact and legend is often thin, sometimes blurred.

Possibly that controversial clergyman Bernard Walke sensed all this and may have found a key to the Arthurian enigma when he said 'I do not know what historical evidence there is for connecting Tintagel with the Holy Grail legend, but I am convinced something of spiritual import happened here.'

MERLIN'S CAVE

Merlin's Cave at Tintagel is full of atmosphere and drama: arguably the most famous cave in all Cornwall. Where better to begin a tour of Arthurian Cornwall?

First, something about Merlin himself.

In both English and French versions it is Merlin who features in Arthur's birth, assists Arthur in obtaining the magical sword Excalibur, and becomes the young man's tutor. Like Arthur, Merlin was seen in the Middle Ages as an *historical* figure.

Merlin's cave lying directly below the Castle ruins, is well worth a visit. It pierces the great cliff, cutting through to a rocky beach on the other side of the headland.

There are two accounts of Arthur's birth. Geoffrey saw it in human detail.

Uther Pendragon, King of Britain, fell in love with Ygraine, wife of Gorlois, Duke of Cornwall, the most beautiful woman in the land. The King's love for her was such that her husband kept her a prisoner at Tintagel. Infuriated, Uther came to Cornwall. Such was his longing for the woman that Merlin, the Wizard, prescribed a magic brew enabling him to look like the twin brother of Gorlois. Thus disguised, he had no difficulty in entering the Castle and that night he slept with Ygraine. As a result Arthur was conceived. Gorlois was defeated and killed in battle with Uther's army, and his wife, now free, became Queen of Britain.

The second version of Arthur's birth is charged with magic and supernatural powers. Some writers have even suggested Arthur was conceived of the gods. Here, at Tintagel it is easy to picture Merlin's acceptance of the babe from the Atlantic.

MERLIN IS something of an enigma. Some chroniclers regard him as a benevolent character – others a more sinister figure. One theory is that Merlin had a human mother but a demonic father – they say the devil was trying to create a Satanic child. But the whole thing misfired; though Merlin retained powers he chose to use them for good rather than evil.

HERE ARE two illustrations of his cave. The dramatic photograph was taken by the late Ronald Youlton, the well-known Tintagel photographer, and the drawing is by Felicity Young, also of Tintagel, familiar to Bossiney readers for a whole range of illustrations and a growing reputation as a Bossiney author.

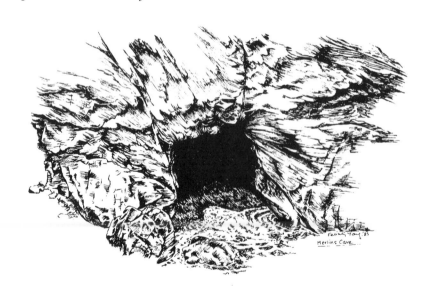

Merlins Cave

TINTAGEL CASTLE

THIS GREAT HEADLAND is thought to have been farmed up until around 350 AD. The farmers, though, left the hillside and when St Juliot, the Celtic missionary, arrived in 500 AD, he found the place deserted.

St Juliot, probably from Wales, quickly established a monastery on the headland: the settlement had running water, libraries and a healing centre; the land was well cultivated and for around 400 years there was prosperity. Then in the ninth century under Saxon rule and because of economic difficulties the monastery went into decline and decay. By the end of the twelfth century when the Normans were tightening their hold on Cornwall, following their arrival in 1067, no trace of St Juliot's monks remained.

Again the headland was uninhabited and the Normans, with a sense of strategy, saw the excellence of Tintagel as a defensive position and fortified it. Tintagel is more than a spectacular setting, it dominates the northern seaboard of Cornwall.

As a medieval stronghold Tintagel Castle would have been of some importance, protecting the land from Irish and Welsh invaders. A royal castle, belonging to the King, and held for him by constables, Tintagel, an out-of-the-way location, served useful purposes: David, Prince of Wales, when in rebellion against the first Edward, took refuge here, and was protected by Richard, Earl of Cornwall. A century later John de Northampton, Lord Mayor of London was brought to Tintagel; '*and for his unruly mairolty condemned thither as a perpetual penetenciary.*'

We do know the castle was kept in some splendour. In 1388 a

The North Gate
Tintagel Castle.

warrant was issued by John Slegh, Keeper of the King's Castle of Tintagel, for the purpose of vestments of rich silk, and altar frontals embroidered with figures of saints.

However, a combination of things worked against the castle: wind, wild weather, and the falling cliffs all slowly and sometimes not so slowly, reduced Tintagel Castle to a ruin; so much so that Leland reported to Henry VIII: *This castel hath been a marvellous strong fortress and almost situ in loco inexpugnabile, especially for the dungeon, that is on a great and terrabil crag environed with the se, but having a drawbridge from the residue of the castel on to it. Shepe now fede within the dungeon.*

Here is how an early travel writer described a visit to the Castle, probably around the turn of the century:

'Great caverns pierce the rocks on either side, the largest completely tunnelling the headland, but this does not make it an island at high tide, though it is often called so.

'We obtain the key of the castle from a cottage close by, and then make the ascent by a precarious path not too well protected with railings. The narrow ledge of the approach we may well imagine to have been the scene of Launcelot's fight with the giants (Le Morte D'Arthur, book vi., chap. xi.).

'*Unlocking the little door we enter the castle. What a bewildering place it is! Almost as perplexing as the legends of Arthur and his knights. The walls are rudely constructed of small stones, with many holes in them, conjectured to have held the beams and scaffolding poles during the building. They would have been filled with clay, which has fallen out in course of ages. The chapel of St Juliot is the most perfect part. It has been carefully traced out, and the granite altar slab is preserved; stone benches remain in the western porch and some fragments of carving have been collected and brought to this spot. Here Merlin was buried, "in a rich sepulchre," shown by an old priest to Launcelot and Gawaine, who tells them, "In this sepulchre was placed the body of Merlin, but never might it be set inside the chapel, wherefore perforce it remaineth outside, and know of very truth that the body lieth not within the sepulchre, for as soon as it was set therein it was taken out and snatched away."*

'*Beyond the chapel, after passing the burying ground on the southern side of the headland, is a picturesque crag known as the Pinnacle Rock. King Arthur's seat, and the "Window" are near this, with small sinkings hollowed in the rock known as his "cups and saucers," and, beyond again, his footprint.*

'*On the mainland traces can be found of the dungeon and castle keep, the latter fairly distinct. The length of the walls gives an impression of the dis-*

Tintagel Castle

15

tance to which the defences on these rocky heights must have extended. In mediaeval times the castle on the mainland was connected with the promontory by a drawbridge. It is believed that much of the cliff between has fallen since the castle was built. The rocks themselves are quite as worthy of consideration as the ruins; they are twisted into contortions or faults by earth-movements in the most remarkable manner, shelving in fantastic lines as they rise above the sea.'

It is an interesting fact that this majestic headland is linked to two great European legends: King Arthur and Tristan and Isolde. The connection between the two is reinforced when some accounts make Tristan a Knight of the Round Table. The late Ronald Duncan, a gifted writer who farmed near Morwenstow, told me how in reading *The Romance of Tristan* by J. Bedier, translated by Hilaire Belloc, he discovered not only a parallel between Arthur and Tristan, but also a kindred spirit, shared by both, with St George. Sitting in his farmhouse kitchen, Ronald reasoned you have Arthur's great prowess in the field *and* Tristan as a slayer of monsters, just as St George slew the dragon.

▶

KIRSTY GARDINER, born in 1971, lives at Lower Trevilla, Feock near Truro. She started writing poems and illustrated stories at the age of eight. She loves drawing and painting. Kirsty has a strong Christian faith and is proud of her long Cornish heritage. She writes songs with her brother Alex who is a pianist and photographer. This is Kirsty's fourth poem for Bossiney. Her previous contributions were 'Cornwall' in *Mysteries of the Cornish Landscape*, by Tamsin Thomas, 'The Scrap Book' in *Old North Cornwall* by Hilda Hambly, and 'Forbidden Ground' in *Mysteries of the South West*, also by Tamsin Thomas.

Of this especially commissioned poem Kirsty says: 'When I started thinking about what Arthur means to so many people I realized they are very interested in his links with their land … the fact that his last knight or remembrancer is the land on which he walked. Somehow I feel the cliffs at Tintagel are the place where it's easiest to imagine how it may perhaps have been …'

THE CLIFF

Perceive me, one last knight,
Waiting for my true king to awake,
To grasp the sword of a thousand battles,
The spells of hatefilled centuries to break,

For I am but a rock of humble wisdom,
Ageless, with no vanity of youth,
My duty is to watch for brothers sleeping,
King Arthur's knights of bravery and truth,

I see the sun that meets the night's moon,
In that magic mirror, Cornwall's sea,
Where they shine an instant, one, together,
That is where Excalibur will be,

That is where the goal for me lies hidden,
Unattainable, as Dozmary Pool cannot taste light,
My sign, my polished, burning symbol,
Borne in heart by Arthur's one last knight,

This history will never die or be forgotten,
History lives in every stone I bear and every grass's blade,
His arms are the branches in this wild and wondrous country,
His skin the soil on which this knight is laid,

I am alive, awake and eternal,
I bear the torch of the King I serve,
For he is sleeping, but he breathes forever,
His pulse is the beating wind to sear the nerve,

I do not forget my King, King Arthur,
Watch over him with eyes set deep in a cold rock face,
For I am the last knight lit by starshine,
My arms, these rocky cliffs, are his resting place.

K.G.

KING ARTHUR'S Great Halls in the main street of Tintagel pictured below – an essential destination on any worthwhile Arthurian tour of the west. And above – just three of the superb stained glass windows at Tintagel. They are fit for a cathedral.

KING ARTHUR'S GREAT HALLS, TINTAGEL

THESE BEAUTIFUL HALLS are an important destination on any tour of King Arthur in the West.

Set in the centre of Tintagel village, this is the home of the Arthurian Experience with Robert Powell, the actor, as Merlin and narrator, taking us on a journey through that curious thing we call Time, telling Arthur's life in laser lights, music and sound.

From here radiates the worldwide Fellowship of the Knights of the Round Table. Everything here is based on the Arthurian romances.

But to begin at the beginning we must go back to a man called Frederick Thomes Glasscock, a millionaire – a partner in the famous custard firm of Monkhouse and Glasscock – he came to Cornwall to retire, but instead, falling in love with the romances and seeing their commercial possibilities, he founded the Fellowship of the Order of the Round Table, and started reaping a second fortune.

Ronald Youlton, a well-known Tintagel personality, who was a neighbour in our Bossiney years, told me how the retired millionaire saw a display of Monkhouse and Glasscock's jellies and custard powders in the window of his father's grocer's shop – a display that also included the sword Excalibur and the Round Table, which first caught the imagination of Frederick Glasscock.

Ronald Youlton recalled: 'He built a small hall at first, about 1930, but when his Fellowship of the Order of the Knights of the Round Table flourished, a larger hall was needed.

'You could join the Order as a Searcher if you were a child. A teenager could be a pilgrim for a small fee. You could then progress through twelve months' probation to qualify as a knight, as long as you were proposed and seconded. You were then presented with a book on the Fellowship and other literature for a small cost.

'The King Arthur business snowballed and on 5 June 1933 over 500 people came from all parts for the opening of the new grand Hall of Chivalry, built behind the earlier King Arthur's Hall. This was consecrated by the Bishop of Truro and Frederick Glasscock was well on the way to making his second million. He went to America and launched the idea successfully over there and on his return had to employ secretaries to deal with the correspondence.'

THE GREAT Granite Throne, each pillar made from a different type of Cornish granite.

Ronald Youlton, who himself started as a Pilgrim in the Order, went on to describe the knighting ceremony: 'The new knight would be suitably attired, while those already knighted wore robes of blue or red according to their rank, whether knights of the sword or sceptre. The principles of the Order were read from a scroll, prayers were said, oaths made. The ceremony started in semi-darkness until the sword Excalibur was drawn from the scabbard with a great flourish and Glasscock – in the role of King Arthur – struck the new knight on the shoulder, giving him his name: Sir Galahad, perhaps, Sir Lancelot, or Sir Bedevere.' There are though no knighting ceremonies these days.

The Arthur story has inspired some fine art over the years. That fact is underlined in the smaller hall where there are ten paintings by William Hatherell RI. These oils, painted in an attractive figurative style, were especially commissioned and are all taken from descriptions in Malory's *Morte d'Arthur*. The paintings and the copies of shields and banners, spears and swords of the knights all combine to generate a powerful atmosphere. Swords, of course, go back hundreds of years before Arthur – not only the swords but their symbolism have featured strongly in folklore and history; swords have even become features of our language: expressions like 'put to the sword' and 'the pen is mightier than the sword.'

But the splendour of the first hall hardly prepares one for the size and grandeur of the second hall.

A paragraph from the excellent *King Arthur's Great Hall of Chivalry*, a guide on sale in the shop at the front, concisely pinpoints the whole philosophy:

'The Hall stands as a central Temple of Chivalry where inspiration can be obtained by all who are interested in reviving that Ideal of Chivalry. This alone will enable the world to live in peace, which should be the foundation and standard of every civilised land, and yet will not interfere with the freedom of any person concerning their nationality or race, religion or creed or political opinion. When the Round Table was made it was said that all the world, Christian and heathen, could meet at it and that it was for all the world to repair unto. Thus was forecast the means by which the Kingdom of God on earth should come to pass, and our hope is that this centre may help to bring about that which is desired by so many.'

This hall is a great joy for any Cornishman or woman. Cornish craftsmen and workers were employed in its building – and they did their work well. Today it is used for Masonic Lodge meetings. Colour and light make great impact, the stones astonishing in their variety: subtle shades, deep contracts.

Inside these walls you begin to understand Cornwall's mineral richness, and the windows are coloured in such a way as to reflect their virtues. These 72 magnificent windows – fit for any cathedral – more than reflect the Knights and their Coats of Arms; those standing for the highest ideals are brightest. Their colours also correspond with the rainbow: purple at one end, golden red at the other, and they are dedicated to those organisations who pursue King Arthur's lofty yet practical ideals.

Lofty yet practical is the Round Table itself, and there is a splendid reproduction of the table here. Some say the Round Table was the inspired idea of a Cornish carpenter. Others believe wise old Merlin saw it as symbolic of the roundness of the world. One ancient source says: *'This Round Table was ordained of Arthur, that when his fair fellowship sat to meat, their chairs should be high alike, their service equal and none before or after his comrade.'* The outer edge of this democratic table apparently stood for eternity and reminded all of their equality.

To stand, as we have done, alongside the Round Table at Tintagel is a reminder of all this – almost enabling us to see the Knights seated around it, their shields hung over their matching seats.

It recalls too another important link: the linking of the Round Table to the Holy Grail. Joseph of Arimathea set up the Grail Table to perpetuate the Last Supper when Judas Iscariot betrayed Christ. That betrayal is why a place was always left empty at the Grail Table. In due course, the Grail Table became the model for the Round Table. Again a vacant place remained – but for different, better, purpose. The Dangerous Seat, as it was known, was only for the ultimate knight – the man who was to win the Holy Grail.

So the Round Table is deeper than democratic dining and equality, it stands for wholeness and the quest for perfection.

ANOTHER highly evocative painting by William Hatherell RI at Tintagel. Sir Lancelot refused sight of the Sangreal – which is another word for the Holy Grail.

For many people standing in this magnificent hall must be a special moment, almost as if they are on hallowed ground. For thousands of visitors this building must have been an awakening, a door opening, an invitation and inspiration to delve deeper into Arthur and related subjects.

I never come here without thinking of Frederick Thomas Glasscock. If he were to come back tomorrow he would be heartened to know his Halls are in good caring hands – and continue to draw people like magnets. Tintagel, the whole of Cornwall for that matter, should be proud of this great asset.

Open for a large part of the year, these Halls remain incredible monuments to a complex character, a millionaire who found his spiritual home on this rugged North Cornish coast.

BOSSINEY MOUND

THE VILLAGE of Bossiney grew around what is today a hump on the landscape. Bossiney Mound, alongside the squat Methodist chapel, just off the coastal road linking Tintagel and Boscastle, has a special place in the Arthurian story in Cornwall. *'According to Cornish tradition,'* said Sabine Baring-Gould, *'King Arthur's Round Table lies deep in the earth under this earthen circular mound; only on Midsummer night does it rise, and then the flash of light from it for a moment illuminates the sky, after which the golden table sinks again ...'*

The mound was, in fact, a castle used for defensive purposes until the building of bigger Tintagel Castle, its architect was Robert, Earl of Mortain, a half-brother of William the Conqueror.

CASTLE-AN-DINAS

WE CAME HERE on a clear morning and all three of us – Felicity, photographer Ray Bishop and me – were all agreed on one thing. If Arthur did use this place it would have been a vital strategic position.

Not for nothing did Daphne du Maurier in her book *Vanishing Cornwall refer to it as 'the finest hill castle in all Cornwall.'*

It was out of season, and we were the only people here. We wondered how many visitors come. Either way, they would need to use their imagination – as we endeavoured to do. You do need a vivid imagination to see it all: the army of warriors, the stabling, the dining chamber and the sleeping quarters. This is the challenge of our Arthurian journeys: our curiosity and imagination are stirred, and Castle-an-Dinas is a good example.

Here is how Tamsin Thomas responded to the setting in her *Mysteries of the South West:*

'Castle-an-Dinas also features in the stories of King Arthur and King Mark, both key figures in the romantic history of Cornwall. Some say the Castle was Arthur's hunting lodge from whence he set forth on horseback to hunt across the wilds of Goss Moor – and before you dismiss this theory with the claim that Arthur was nothing more than a fanciful legend, let me tell you there are growing numbers of people who firmly believe he must have existed for history to have gone the way it has in Cornwall.'

Some deserted places have that long-forgotten feel. It is almost as if the men and women who lived and worked in them have somehow failed to leave any definite recorded history. Yet such places have a compulsion about them. They encourage us to make a pilgrimage – Castle-an-Dinas is such a spot.

CASTLE-AN-DINAS: *This hill castle must have been an important strategic location, commanding views for miles and miles across the varied Cornish landscape.* SLAUGHTER BRIDGE *near Camelford. Did Arthur fight his last battle hereabouts? It is interesting to speculate how and why the bridge got such a name.*

SLAUGHTER BRIDGE

THERE ARE BIGGER, more beautiful bridges than Slaughter Bridge, near Camelford, but it is an essential part of any Arthurian tour of Cornwall.

Very old, not arched but but built over flat stones on piers, it has an affinity with that celebrated clapper Postbridge on Dartmoor. Here we meet the River Camel in its infancy and the Camel hereabouts is said – by some – to have been the battlefield of Camlann, Arthur's last battle when he was forced to fight his bastard son Mordred who had betrayed him – a bitter and bloody battle. At the end of it only two knights of the Round Table survived.

The Once and Future King knew his time had come. 'I am come to mine end,' he declared, and he killed Mordred with a spear, but the dying Mordred had enough strength to raise his sword and strike his father on the head piercing through his helmet.

Upstream in a nook lies a stone with moss and strange lettering. Here in Cornwall we call it Arthur's grave, but it is more likely to be that of a Celtic chieftain. If this stone does recall some ancient battle then it is likely to have been around 825 during the Saxon Conquest of Kernow.

The battle however lives on in a poem by the twelfth century priest Layamon:

On the River Camel, they came together
The place was called Camelford. May the name last forever
And at Camelford were gathered sixty thousand
And more. Mordred was their leader.
And the noble Arthur rode there

With a huge army, although it was doomed.
On the River Camel, they fought together,
Raised standards, massed them together,
Sparks flew out, spears shattered
Shields broke, shafts snapped
The mighty host fought together there.
The Camel was in flood with measureless blood.

THE MAGICAL sword Excalibur in anvil: an exhibit at King Arthur's Halls evocative of the knightly battles Arthur's army fought in the West.

KING ARTHUR'S HALL

HERE ON Bodmin Moor when we walk or ride across the downs that bear the great King's name, we are not only travelling across a beautiful stretch of moorland – we are in the middle of a Cornish mystery.

This is an ancient landscape: a strange, sometimes menacing beauty. Out here on King Arthur's Downs, you feel you are somehow on the edge of distant history, memories, memorials of the other earlier people surround you: an almost haunting sensation.

Why King Arthur's Downs?

The question is inevitable – unanswerable.

In a curious way, the Downs are more a feeling than a place. There's an indefinable something: a kind of magic. King Arthur's Downs have that quality which can be felt – only now and then – in the work of great creative spirits: that sense of 'something more' beyond the tangible and the visible.

You cannot use words like nice or pretty about this place. Perceptive Tamsin Thomas touched on this aspect in her *Mysteries of the Cornish Landscape*: '*I tend to favour the idea that if there were such a king, he was a hardened fighter, popular with the women and well travelled, and not a knight in shining armour astride a majestic grey stallion. The "rough diamond" image would fit better with the landscape ...*'

And when we come to King Arthur's Hall, the questioning begins again.

The difficult truth is nobody knows *when* these banks were built – or *why*. They stand alone, rectangular on the skyline of the moor, approximately fifty yards along and roughly a cricket pitch – twenty-two yards – in width. Today they are weathered down to the height of the average jockey. Today, too, the interior is marginally lower than the surrounding moorscape, and partly under water.

Inside King Arthur's Hall, large stones were set up on end as a retaining wall, something like sixty are still in position. With the weathering of the bank beyond, they now stand freely, like gaunt sculptures created by Nature and the thing we call time, somehow generating the impression we are standing inside some primitive temple – and maybe we are doing just that.

ANCIENT STONES which guard a secret – did King Arthur come here? Did he and his armies gather in this remote place? – or is it just another of the many prehistoric monuments to be found in Cornwall?

DECEMBER SHADOWS cast by the stones of King Arthur's Hall, captured by photographer Barry Englefield.

ARTHUR'S QUOIT

ARTHUR'S QUOIT near Minions on the eastern edge of Bodmin Moor is another Cornish mystery and rarity. First, why Arthur's? Was he here? This magnificent monument to some distant dynasty had two burial chambers. Only that fine quoit down at Zennor in West Penwith can boast a second chamber in all Cornwall. Responsible researchers into the past believe it was probably built and used as a dual tomb circa 1800-1100 BC.

DOZMARY POOL

WATER somehow gives moorland a certain vitality. There is an energising quality. Interestingly, too, many ancient tales feature the sea, a river or a lake.

Standing on the rim of Dozmary you understand that breadth and space are dominant features in many of our Cornish landscapes – relying on basic elements of water, earth and sky. A mile in circumference, Dozmary Pool is a place of changing mood and beauty: a place of mystery and magic. The old people had an idea it was bottomless. In reality, Dozmary is surprisingly shallow. Often the pool becomes a mirror reflecting the forms of moor and cloud.

Some say Dozmary is where Sir Bedivere reluctantly threw away the magical sword Excalibur. Following that last terrible battle, Sir Bedivere carried the dying king away from the battlefield – and Arthur instructed that the sword be thrown into a stretch of water nearby. Bedivere hated the idea of throwing away Excalibur, and hid it instead. When he returned to Arthur, the King asked 'What happened in the water?' 'Nothing,' replied the knight. Arthur, knowing he had been disobeyed, repeated his order. For a second time Bedivere hesitated, but the third time he did as he was asked. He threw the magical sword: *there came an arm and a hand, and took it and cleight (seized) it, and shook it thrice and brandished, and then vanished with the sword into the water.*

Here at Dozmary we are reminded of Morgan Le Fay, Arthur's half-sister and the ruler of the enchanted island of Avalon where Arthur was taken for the treatment of his wounds after that final battle.

Morgan Le Fay had the powers of an enchantress – and those powers included the ability to transform herself into a bird, all of which leads us on to the Cornish Chough. The real Cornish Chough sadly became extinct, but Choughs, from outside Kernow, have been reintroduced: an important fact because, according to the superstitious Cornish, when the Cornish Chough goes, Cornwall's prosperity will go with the bird. However, there is a ray of hope because deep back in Cornish folklore is the theory that Arthur did not die in that bloody battle at Slaughter Bridge – instead the Chough incarnated the King's soul – and Arthur will come again.

LOE POOL

FROM Dozmary to Loe Pool is to move from one Cornish lake to another – and to go deep into Arthurian rivalry. Not all claim Dozmary as the spot where Excalibur said 'good-bye' to this world. Some believed Loe Pool, approximately one mile south of Helston, is the more likely location. Here we see the largest lake in all Cornwall, once described by the late Sir John Betjeman as 'a sort of Chesil Beach with a fresh water lagoon behind it.'

Whichever location it was, the tale fired the creativity of the great Tennyson whose epic poem *Idylls of the King* is one of the great landmarks in Arthurian literature:

… the sword
That rose from out the bosom of the lake,
And Arthur row'd across and took it – rich
With jewels, elfin Urim, on the hilt,
Bewildering heart and eye – the blade so bright
That men are blinded by it …

GUINEVERE

IT IS AN odd fact that whereas there are Arthur place names in the west, there is no Guinevere location. She is, of course, a central character as Queen, and it was her relationship with Lancelot that wrecked Camelot.

The collapse of Camelot was brought about by 'the weakness of human nature, by the sensual overcoming the spiritual.' Interestingly in this century John F Kennedy, as the President of the United States, created *his* Court of Camelot at the White House – and some shrewd political commentators believe that Bill Clinton, elected President in 1992, will in turn create *his* Camelot. So the Arthur spirit continues way into our times.

If there are Merlin places, then it is even more baffling to find no sites linked to Arthur's queen. There is, though, a splendidly detailed painting of Guinevere by William Morris, with Jane Burden, soon afterwards to become his wife, as the model. It shows her disrobing in the bed chamber with a tiny pet dog curled up on the bed! There is also a poignant illustration by Doré of the parting of Guinevere and Lancelot in *The Idylls of the King*.

An interesting legacy to the queen is, in some Westcountry villages people will refer to a certain kind of girl or young woman as 'a right little Guinevere'. The adjective, though, may be wrong because William Morris's painting portrays a queen of some height, and, of course, Vanessa Redgrave, chosen to play Guinevere in the film *Camelot*, is a tall actress – an interesting choice, too, in that she is strong and dramatic.

MERLYN'S ROCK

NOW WE COME down to West Cornwall, to Mousehole which sounds like something out of Beatrix Potter. It is, in fact, a fishing village three miles south of Penzance – Mou'zl is the pronunciation – granite quays, the cry of sea gulls, a jigsaw of cobbled courtyards and narrow winding streets.

Merlin's name lives on here in the form of a rock just off Mousehole – Merlyn spelt with a y in Cornish. There's an ancient Penwith tradition that the wizard made an uncanny forecast about the village; '. . . strangers will land on the rock of Merlin who will burn Mousehole.' And in 1595 invading Spaniards did just that. Seeking revenge for the defeat of their Armada, the Spaniards turned the village into a terrible furnace.

Like many prophets Merlin may have been able to 'see' for others but not for himself. He fell in love with an enchantress by the name of Nimue, but she tired of him. Casting a spell on him, Nimue banished him to a curious imprisonment; confining him to a cave for the rest of time.

LANYON QUOIT
near MADRON

LANYON MUST BE one of the most photographed monuments in ancient Kernow. Looking rather like a grand dining
table shaped by some giant long ago it has a definite place in the
Arthurian tapestry; according to legend King Arthur dined here on
the eve of his last battle and Merlin predicted the King and his
commanders would assemble here just once more – before the end
of the world.

TABLE-MEN at Sennen: the setting for another Merlin prediction.

TABLE-MEN, SENNEN

THERE IS another dining story down in the Parish of Sennen hard by Land's End.

Table-Men, which means Rock Table, also claims a strange prophecy. This large flat stone is said to have been where the seven Saxon Kings dined together, and Merlin added to speculation by predicting that even more Kings will gather around Table-Men before some impressive event – or the end of the world.

THE ISLES OF SCILLY

OUR TOUR OF sites relating to Arthur now take us off the mainland of Cornwall. Twenty-eight miles west of Land's End are the Isles of Scilly. Here we encounter two islets known as Great and Little Arthur.

According to the ancient story-tellers Lyonesse was above water during the days of the Once and Future King. In fact some researchers say the Scillies are the high peaks of Lyonesse.

Following that final conflict with Mordred, Arthur's men fled westward, towards the setting sun, and once they had got beyond Lyonesse, Merlin, by his strange powers, stirred an earthquake, engulfing Mordred's followers as Lyonesse drowned. As a result Arthur's contingent escaped to the Fortunate Isles.

Fellow Bossiney author Brenda Duxbury in our companion title *King Arthur Country in Cornwall* told how she and her sailor husband Ken experienced their journey beyond Land's End.

'If you sail to Scilly into the setting sun, you will no doubt feel as we did, that this stretch of water is like a moat, separating the world of everyday from that other magical world.

'Legend in Greek and Roman times spoke of a group of islands beyond the Pillars of Hercules called the Islands of the Blest, where life was idyllic and where heroes were brought to be buried in order to find eternal peace. This idea is presented in Celtic myth and their land of the dead, or Avalon, has been linked with the Scillies, the Land of the Shades, where holy men inhabited the islands and a chief or king could be safely buried and remain in peace.'

BLACKINGSTONE ROCK, DEVON

IT IS A curious fact that whereas Cornwall and Somerset are littered with Arthurian locations, the King scarcely gets a mention in the landscape which divides the two.

If Arthur's were a roving role in the West, then this gap is even more puzzling because in his to-ing and fro-ing between Somerset and Cornwall he would have frequently journeyed through the land we know today as Devon.

However, we do find one definite Devon location: Blackingstone Rock near Moretonhampstead. Here, it is said, Arthur met and fought with no less than the Devil himself. Satan, the supreme spirit of evil, would have been a formidable opponent. The Devil does, in fact crop up in a number of Devon stories.

It was in February 1855 that a baffling trail of hoofprints were found on snow in South Devon. In a straight line they stretched for almost one hundred miles around the Teignmouth, Dawlish and Exmouth areas. More than 130 years on, they remain a Devon mystery and are often referred to as the Devil's hoofprints.

ARTHUR IN DORSET

WAS ARTHUR in Dorset? One man who has no doubts, is
Barney Camfield, the well-known healer, lecturer and broad-
caster who lives at Alphington near Exeter. In *Dorset Mysteries*, published by Bossiney in 1989, Barney contributed a chapter entitled
'Arthur in Dorset'. At this point we had better explain Barney
bases his conviction on psycho-expansion which is a form of time
travel. The cynic, of course, will scoff. We merely say that for those
who accept reincarnation then psycho-expansion is natural in that
it is a return to an earlier life.

Towards the end of his chapter Barney Camfield wrote:

'*We had been around Cerne Abbas and had gone on to Minterne Magna
two miles north. It was nearby that Arthur had been born, in a wooden
house now long gone. But immediately after birth he had been taken to the
spring, a few yards away, for his 'blessing'. His mother was a beautiful
golden haired woman. She was of Romano-British descent – as were many
of the chiefs and others of the aristocracy of the day – hence their knowledge
of Latin kept up by the Christian priests of course. She had come to a safe
area to be with a relative – maybe a sister – and there she delivered Aries -
born Arthur.*

'*We had found where the spring had then sprung, in a copse. If you look
where the four roads meet, travelling north on the A352 half a mile or so
from Minterne Magna and a couple of yards up on the right of the right
hand road – which says it is unfit for motor vehicles – you'll find some
stone steps – Victorian I would say – up the bank into a triangular copse
(OS Sheet 104; 657/053). There indeed are the earthworks. And look to
your left as Arthur did that afternoon and you'll see a hill close by. "It's
there. That's where I'm buried," said he.*'

WE FEEL Dorset – parts of it anyway – has a distinctly Arthurian atmo-sphere.

43

Journeying on ...

NOW IS the time for FELICITY YOUNG to take the baton.

You could not have a better, more thoughtful, travelling companion. As an illustrator and a painter, Felicity's work reflects great attention to detail: every stone, each shadow and, as a writer, she researches diligently.

So thorough is Felicity's approach that I am reminded of some words by R.M. Laing: '*In this particular type of journey, the direction we have to take is back in, because it was way back that we started to go down and out ... we have a long, long way to go back to contact the reality ...*'

We have travelled together on many Bossiney expeditions and it is always a pleasure. She is not only perceptive and naturally curious, she somehow encourages you to look at things from a different angle and sometimes see them in a new light.

Felicity is a born traveller – never happier I suspect than when seeing life from the saddle. But whether she is riding, walking, cycling or travelling in a car she is conscious of transition, between the known and the unknown, the past and the present. Travelling with her sharpens your awareness. That has been my experience. I hope it is yours.

M.W.

About the Author ...

FELICITY YOUNG *is a Cornish-based painter who lives at Tintagel with her husband Ian, daughter Hazel, horse Red and dogs Arthur and Digger. She lived in Somerset for more than 20 years and still makes regular visits to the county: an ideal background for anyone writing about Arthurian sites in the West. She was educated at Lord Digby's Grammar School, Sherborne, Dorset.*

Since 1984 she has contributed more than 300 illustrations for a whole range of Bossiney titles and has done a radio broadcast on the craft of illustrating books.

In 1989 Felicity made her debut as a Bossiney author, contributing a chapter on Lawrence of Arabia in Dorset Mysteries. *Then in 1990 came her first book:* Curiosities of Exmoor. *In 1991 she contributed a chapter in* Strange Dorset Stories, *and in 1992 she explored 'Strange Places', a chapter in* Strange Stories of Cornwall.

Now she writes about Arthur places in Somerset and Avon and produces many of the illustrations.

THE RIVER CAM
AND QUEEN CAMEL

THE STORY tells us that Arthur fought his last battle at Camlann, here he was fatally wounded by the evil Mordred:

'When Arthur rang'd his red-cross ranks
On conscious Camlan's crimsoned banks;
My Mordred's faithless guile decreed
Beneath a Saxon spear to bleed!'

(Thomas Warton)

Speculation continues as to the site of this dramatic encounter, but Somerset has come up with its own answer. Not far from Cadbury Castle is the village of Queen Camel. Driving through the winding street, surrounded by clusters of delightful houses you cross a narrow packhorse bridge, which spans the River Cam. Coincidence maybe, or could this meandering little tributary of the great river Yeo be the actual site of Arthur's final battle? But it was Queen Eleanor, wife of Edward I who owned the estate in the thirteenth century who lent her name to this picturesque village not Queen Guinevere.

If the legend is true, Arthur was borne away to the Isle of Avalon (Glastonbury) not many miles as the crow flies, from the river Cam by boat. He was accompanied by three 'dark queens' whom Sir Thomas Mallory identified as: *'Arthur's sister, Queen Morgan le Fay; the other was the Queen of North Galis; the third was the Queen of the Waste Lands.'* Arthur instructed Sir Bedivere to take the sword Excalibur: *'and go with it to yonder water side, and when thou comest there I charge thee throw my sword into that watter ...'*

It is thought that the water in question is the River Brue at

Pomparles Bridge which I mention in a separate chapter, on the
busy road from Glastonbury to Bridgewater. Not a very romantic
setting but looking at this stretch of water which sometimes forms
a lake after rain, covering nearby fields, there is a hint of credibili-

ty; this area may well have been underwater in Arthur's time.

This theory conflicts with the Cornish claim that Arthur fell in battle at Slaughterbridge near Camelford, their site of Camlann, Dozmary Pool on Bodmin Moor the lake into which Excalibur was thrown. In 1190 a grave was unearthed in the grounds of Glastonbury which the monks proclaimed to be Arthur's grave. This must surely swing the pendulum back in Somerset's favour as having a rightful claim on the great king. Malory tells us that the three queens took Arthur to Avalon … *'these ladies brought him to his grave.'*

So perhaps Avalon is, after all, Glastonbury. If we follow in the wake of Arthur then our next stop along the way must surely be the mystical town of Glastonbury itself.

GLASTONBURY ABBEY

IF IT IS the search for Arthur that brings you to Glastonbury Abbey then once here, the majesty of the ruins will surely make you want to spend more time than it takes for just a quick glance at the site of Arthur's grave.

The Abbey ruins, set among well-mown lawns and imposing trees, are all that remain of one of medieval England's greatest monasteries. The broken shell, left standing in silent splendour, attracts thousands of visitors each year, but for all the attention there is still an atmosphere of tranquility and peace which drifts around the disfigured structure reflecting the glory of a bygone age.

None of the walls still standing is older than 1184. On May 24 that year a great fire destroyed the monastery – very sad to think that so many valuable and beautiful treasures were reduced to ashes, never to be see again. It must have broken the hearts of the monks to see the devastation of their wondrous buildings, the books, gold and silver ornaments, gone for ever.

The history of the Abbey prior to this date, is a little sketchy. It is believed this place was the home of the first Christian community in England. Monks and hermits may have lived here as early as the fifth and sixth centuries. During the Saxon invasion it remained a stronghold of Christianity. Without the original buildings to give clues, the writings of William of Malmesbury, a monastic librarian and leading historian of his time, have been of great interest.

At the invitation of the monks, William, who was a local man, composed a book on the church of Glastonbury, unravelling the

records to show the connections with some of the greatest Saints. He hints that the original old church of St Mary on the abbey site, a crude affair made of wattle-work with timber reinforcements and a casing of lead may have been built by 'disciples of Christ' in the first century. It was from this sprang the belief that Joseph of Arimathea came to Glastonbury. Though William himself never made a claim as such, the story was taken up by Robert de Boron, a French poet, in his tale about the Grail coming to Avalon and Joseph was named as the leader of the founding group of disciples.

The Lady Chapel stands today where the Old Church dedicated to the Virgin Mary once stood. In 1500 Abbot Beere dug out a crypt beneath it, creating a shrine to Joseph, he also went so far as to create a new coat of arms made up of a cross made from a sprouting staff and two cruet cups, thus deeply entrenching the tradition that Joseph had indeed, as Grail bearer, come to Britain and, more important, to Glastonbury.

THE ABBEY at Glastonbury has historic connections with many saints and holy men, and its associations with the Grail link it to Arthur.

ARTHUR'S BRIDGE

ON THE road between Castle Cary and Shepton Mallet, near the turning for the lovely Somerset village of Ditcheat, is a bridge named after our hero. Arthur's Bridge, crossing the River Alham, a tributary of the Brue, is unremarkable but it offers yet more proof of the strong belief that Arthur did travel widely in Somerset.

I can remember as a young girl frequently passing by the sign at the roadside. I would conjure up visions of the king with his knights beside him, their armour glinting in the sunlight as they crossed the river at this spot. Here the fields are flat and fertile, cows browse contentedly in their pastures. It is a typical rural scene. Where would these gallant men have been travelling?

I often imagined them on their way to some battle or perhaps returning to nearby Cadbury the site of Arthur's court, Camelot where Queen Guinevere awaited her king or maybe her secret love, Lancelot. Fanciful no doubt, as we know Arthur was no medieval king, but I'm certain this is how many people imagine him. Not until we start searching for the 'real' Arthur do we discover the true historical setting for his life, not as glamorous perhaps. but still very evocative.

VISIONS OF the king with his knights beside him, their armour glinting in the sunlight…

THE HUNTING
CAUSEWAY

THERE ARE many ghostly sightings around Cadbury, signifi-cant perhaps as some say this was the site of Arthur's court – Camelot. Below Cadbury Castle lie traces of an ancient track stretching away towards Glastonbury.

The causeway may have been used by Arthur and his knights travelling to and from Camelot. In fact on winter nights it is said they ride from the hill along the causeway to go hunting. Those who claim to have seen this fearsome sight say the tips of their lances glowing in the dark and the baying of the hounds causes the spine to tingle.

The pretty Somerset villages of North and South Barrow are believed to be on the line of the Hunting Causeway, peaceful and unspoilt, they are the epitome of rural tranquility.

IS BATH
'MOUNT BADON'?

TRADITIONALLY King Arthur fought twelve important battles. The historian, Nennius, whose works influenced the twelfth century writer Geoffrey of Monmouth, described each of them, but only one battle can actually be proved real.

This was the battle at Mount Badon. Even though the battle was real enough its site has been a matter of speculation. It is widely agreed the site is in the south west, but beyond that nobody is certain.

One proposed place is near Bath. Solsbury Hillfort, above Batheaston, has long been a strong contender for the site of Arthur's most prestigious battle. With the aid of his mighty sword Excalibur he fought a noble battle against the Saxon invaders, slaughtering, some say, 960 men.

Was this hill within sight of the famous Roman City of Bath the battlefield? Did such carnage take place here? It all seems too peaceful, but then so do many other scenes of death and destruction. Has the landscape masked the horror? It is said Arthur defended his land against the barbaric Saxons in a siege lasting three days and three nights.

GLASTONBURY ZODIAC

I HAVE always felt the streets of Glastonbury are 'friendly'. I was a teenager in the sixties and I suppose a little of the 'flower power' scene which affected all towns, particularly Glastonbury, rubbed off on me. I'm sure the reasons behind this 'feeling' go back a lot further, but this was my first impression of the mystical side of this town.

I clearly remember a mural painted on the wall of one of the many small shops. It was of brightly painted flowers which to me summed up the whole era.

Glastonbury has been a Mecca for people from all walks of life for hundreds of years. In the sixties the hippies were on the trail of love and peace, today the search continues, 'New Age' travellers still flock to this area drawn by Glastonbury's magnetism. There are so many unexplained mysteries here, one particularly great puzzle being the Glastonbury zodiac.

Discovered – if that is the right word – in the early 1920s by sculptor Katherine Maltwood, it is a huge zodiac with the twelve astrological signs drawn within a circle, ten miles in diameter, all super-imposed on the countryside surrounding Glastonbury. Katherine Maltwood had studied the Arthurian legends and was asked to illustrate a book: *The High History of the Holy Grail* which chronicled the travels of knights in search of the Grail.

While preparing her illustrations she discovered that, when plotting the journeys of the knights, she could trace the shape of a lion using landmarks such as the River Cary and Somerton Lane. She consulted a friend who happened to be an astrologer to see if he

THE RUINS of Glastonbury attract people from all walks of life, some browse casually, others, like Katherine Maltwood discover an all absorbing passion which still excites and intrigues others.

could unravel the mystery. He suggested the lion might be Leo and the figure of a man that Katherine had also found could be part of the sign of the twins, Gemini.

Katherine's imagination was fired by this revelation and she worked on to map out the twelve zodiac signs. The Somerset landscape around Glastonbury held the key to a remarkable puzzle. Yet another intriguing link with Arthur, Avalon and Glastonbury appears; it has long been thought that the Round Table represented the Zodiac, perhaps here is another clue ... or maybe a red herring?

Katherine Maltwood published her theory in 1935 in *Glastonbury's Temple of the Stars*. This subject has been the cause of much contention both among sceptics and the more open-minded, but it has nevertheless remained a great Glastonbury mystery. After all, the features have been constant for centuries, whilst the surrounding landscape is continuously in a state of change. With the dawning of the age of Aquarius – to quote that well known song – it is no wonder that travellers converge on this 'Island'. This once-pagan sanctuary is full of mystery and enigma.

POMPARLES BRIDGE

L EAVING Glastonbury and driving towards Street, the hub of the Clarks shoe industry, along the busy A39, there is a bridge which spans the River Brue. Called Pomparles Bridge or the Bridge Perilous, it is supposed to be the place from which the sword Excalibur was cast into the lake.

It is not difficult to imagine this spot as once a huge lake. The levels often flood; the terrain is flat and featureless and after heavy rain the whole area becomes submerged. The Isle of Avalon of the legends was the mystical place where we are told Excalibur was forged. In reality, Glastonbury and its cluster of hills was at one time surrounded by water, and stood just like an island, approachable by boat. It seems feasible that Arthur was carried here by '... *yon dark Queens in yon black boat*' to his final resting place.

We remember that Arthur entrusted Sir Bedivere with his sword Excalibur and bade him throw it into the lake. Bedivere, reluctant to do this, returned to the wounded Arthur and lied that he had done as the king asked. Arthur knew he was lying and repeated his request; on the third occasion Bedivere finally went to the water's edge and he threw the sword as far into the lake as he could; '*and there came an arm and a hand above the water and met it, and clasped it, and so shook it thrice and brandished, and then vanished with the sword in the water.*'

(Malory – Morte D'Arthur)

LINKS

MUCH OF my youth was spent at Pilton, a small village only a few miles from Glastonbury, in the shadow of the Tor. When I married, my connection with Arthur became stronger, my husband, Ian, had lived in Tintagel most of his life, and we were frequent visitors to the place. After a few years of married life we decided to uproot ourselves from Somerset and return to Tintagel where we have now lived since 1982. Ian always had this strong desire, as do many other Tintagel people, to return 'home'. Whether it is the draw of the sea or the friendliness of the place or some other more powerful force, Tintagel certainly has a hold on its community. These two places, Glastonbury and Tintagel, lynch pins in the Arthurian legends, have thus played a very personal role in my life. I have lived close to King Arthur for so many years!

Links often appear as conflicting claims of Arthur having been at two places at the same time. There is much speculation as to the location of his death and his grave. One theory is that he was buried in an unmarked grave, another suggests he was buried in Glastonbury abbey. The final battle where he was fatally wounded, the battle of Camlann, has been attributed to both Slaughterbridge, in Cornwall and a site near Queen Camel in Somerset. So the contest goes on, everyone wanting a share of the glorious warrior. If we search deeper it is possible to find factual rather than speculative connections. One example of this is Cadbury Castle here in Somerset.

At South Cadbury, within sight of Glastonbury Tor, rises the equally commanding feature of the hill fort known as Cadbury

Castle. Five hundred feet above sea level this ancient hill was no medieval castle but massive earthwork ramparts enclosing the huge site of a village covering the central plateau. For a long time, perhaps further back in history, before 1542, when John Leland wrote *'at the very south end of the church of South-Cadbyri standeth Cammallate, sometime a famous town or castle ...'* this special place has been earmarked as Arthur's court – Camelot.

The lane leading up to the hilltop is rough underfoot, it climbs gently upwards through an avenue of majestic trees which in summer touch their leaves together high above your head to form a natural corridor. When you reach the summit a grassy plateau awaits, and a view to rival that of any in Somerset.

It was known already that the eighteen-acre site had been occupied in pre-Roman times but in the mid 1950s the archaeologist Mary Harfield was walking her dog over the ploughed hilltop and discovered pottery fragments and flints. These were examined by C.A. Raleigh Radford (who was responsible for the excavations at Tintagel) and identified as pieces of imported ware from the post-Roman 'Arthur' period.

Here, then, was a strong link between Tintagel Castle, Cornwall and the Cadbury, Glastonbury sites of Somerset. The same expensive goods which came from abroad had been used by a people of some wealth and standing, here at Cadbury as they had been at Tintagel. The hilltop was excavated by Leslie Alcock between 1966 and 1970 and many interesting finds came to light in the area on the highest part of the hill known as Arthur's Palace. It became obvious that Cadbury had been at one time a stronghold of great importance, revamped from its original pre-Roman state and turned into a fortress. Historically the evidence is stacked in favour of this being the site of Arthur's court.

It is said that on Midsummer's Eve or Midsummer's Night, (or even Christmas Eve, no one is absolutely sure!) – Arthur's ghost, accompanied by his phantom knights, rides over the top of the hill and down through the spot where the gatehouse once stood. the purpose of this sortie is unknown but the riders are said then to descend the narrow path which leads to the village of Sutton Montis. With bridles and harness jangling, they proceed through

CADBURY FORT – is this Camelot, Arthur's citadel?

the hamlet finally stopping to allow their horses to drink at a well.

Legends of Arthur abound hereabouts which can only strengthen the feeling that there is no smoke without fire. The romantic

CADBURY CASTLE rises above the surrounding countryside.

vision of the court of Camelot with Arthur and the beautiful Guinevere is particularly strong here. When we are aware that there once stood a large timber hall on the summit known locally as Arthur's Palace since as long ago as 1586, it is easy to let the imagination wander. Was this the great hall where Arthur and his queen held their wedding feast, where the legends of the king and his knights were born? The best way to answer some of these questions is to walk to the top of Cadbury hill, stand and absorb the atmosphere.

Iron Age man first settled here and fortified it – the Romans finally stormed and captured it, eventually Cadbury took shape as a sophisticated fortress; throughout the centuries the labours of man have left their mark on this impressive hill in Somerset. Camelot may be just a legendary place but every so often history crops up with the odd hint, keeping us firmly on the trail of Arthur *and* his court.

THE FORTIFICATIONS, begun in the Iron Age, were massively rein-forced about the time of Arthur.
THE WOODS were part of the ditch and bank defence.

63

GLASTONBURY TOR

TOR IS an old Westcountry word meaning hill. It is difficult to imagine Glastonbury Tor without its distinctive tower – it is such a familiar sight. But until Norman times, when a chapel was built dedicated to St Michael, the hill was bare. The chapel was destroyed by an earthquake in 1275 and lay in ruins for some fifty years until it was rebuilt by the then abbot of Glastonbury, Adam of Sodbury. In the fifteenth century a tower was added to the chapel and this is now all that remains: one of the most intriguing sights in all Somerset. Romantic connections with King Arthur have deemed this place, together with the cluster of hills around Glastonbury, to be the Isle of Avalon.

There can be few more magical sights than that of Glastonbury Tor on a misty October morning. The flat mist-shrouded plain of the Somerset Levels, suddenly interrupted by the almost pyramid-shaped hill, appears like an island floating mysteriously in the patches of bright autumn sunshine. The view from the top of the tor is equally stunning, almost like being on the flight deck of an aeroplane, looking down on to the cloud from above. The climb to the top of the tor is exhausting, made only slightly easier by some steps cut into the steeper, muddier parts. But it is well worth the effort, once at the summit the view is simply breath-taking. In clear weather the Vale of Avalon stretches out below flat and fea-tureless, the Quantock hills and Exmoor appear away in the dis-tance, to the north are the Mendips, beneath which lies Wookey Hole where a bothersome witch is supposed to have been turned into a stalagmite by a Glastonbury monk, and if you know where to

look, you can pick out the dark wooded hilltop of Cadbury, King Arthur's Camelot.

St Michael's Tower which dominates this summit, is the centre of great attention at the time of the summer solstice. Travellers converge here to watch the sunrise, to celebrate this pagan ritual, as hundreds gather in similar fashion at Stonehenge. The belief that the tor is a sacred place is a long-standing one. It is significantly positioned on two major ley lines, the invisible lines said to link places of metaphysical force. Most of the place which are on ley lines are also prominent, suggesting they were used for navigation, but it would be hard to ignore the strength of the mystical power which pervades these sites. One ley line passes through Glastonbury and on to Stonehenge, the other stretches from St Michael's Mount in Cornwall through the tor and on to the stone circles at Avebury in Wiltshire.

There is immense speculation surrounding the formation of the tor, whether it be man-made or natural, logical or magical. The tor is spoken of in legend as being hollow, harbouring a cave. This cave was the palace of King Gwyn, Lord of the Underworld. The tales continue with stories of subterranean waterways and tunnels connecting the tor to the abbey. One of the strongest theories that still remains inconclusive is that of the Tor Maze. The maze refers to the strange pattern of terraces which surround the tor, paths circle the hill forming a spiralling, labyrinth-like pattern similar to those found in Crete, Italy and Ireland and correspond to the two maze carvings on a stone at Rocky Valley near Tintagel, North Cornwall.

This intriguing theory that the terraces are a maze was put forward by an Irishman, Geoffrey Russell in the 1960s. He made detailed models to support his case but unfortunately he was not altogether convincing. Philip Rahtz, the archaeologist, excavated the summit in 1964 but again the theory was not proved. Evidence of habitation during the sixth century AD did come to light however; perhaps here is a link with the oldest known story of Arthur and Glastonbury. In 1130 a Welsh monk Caradoc of Llancarfan whilst writing about the life of St Gildas, tells of Melwas, the ruler of Somerset, carrying off Guinevere, Arthur's wife, and holding her at Glastonbury. Arthur brought troops from Devon and Cornwall to rescue her but the episode was settled by peaceful negotiation and Arthur's lady returned.

Could the archaeological finds on the tor be the remains of an outpost where Melwas held Guinevere? Romantic ideas indeed and not much to substantiate them but whether just fancy or not the tor still holds great mystery, the terraces could have been for agricultural purposes or the remnants of a ritual pathway. We can fantasize about the presence of demons and fairies. As with all legend and folklore, fact and fiction blend into confusion, their roots lying far back in ancient history.

According to the Arthurian legends the King, mortally wounded at the battle of Camlann, betrayed by his bastard son Mordred, was laid in a barge and taken to the Isle of Avalon: *'a pleasant and delightful place and very peaceful'*. This was to be his final resting place or was it? ... Some believed he had not died but would return again, a kind of Celtic Messiah. In a way King Arthur has

THE HOSTAGE QUEEN – Guinevere was held at Glastonbury by King Melwas.

become immortal through legend.

The landscape surrounding Glastonbury Tor is very interesting and puts into perspective the theory behind the idea that Arthur was brought to Avalon by boat. Thousands of years ago the low-lying peat moors were submerged beneath the sea. Evidence of prehistoric man has been preserved in the layers of peat which have accumulated over thousands of years, dating habitation of the Levels as long ago as 4000BC. Much later, around 400BC two settlements grew up, these were the famous Lake Villages of Glastonbury and Meare. They were discovered and excavated by Arthur Bulleid in 1892.

The two villages were rich in information about the prehistoric occupation of the Levels, a vital and unique archaeological record preserved naturally in peat. A change to the environment meant that these settlements were abandoned. By 400AD sea water once again covered parts of the moor, this would certainly bring credibility to the story of the wounded Arthur being ferried by barge across the water to Avalon. Even now, after very heavy rainfall, the Levels can become flooded giving us a glimpse of how life may have been hundreds of years ago.

HILLTOP TO HILLTOP communication would have been easy in Arthur's day. Watchers at Cadbury Castle, 12 miles from Glastonbury Tor could have received and responded to signals within minutes.

BRENT KNOLL

T HE THUNDERING motorway travelling northwards from Bridgwater has a useful milestone by which drivers can gauge their progress. Anyone who travels this road will know Brent Knoll: a strange hill rising out of the flat landscape near the coast of the Bristol Channel. It is highly visible from many places but most importantly from Cadbury and Glastonbury Tor. It may have been a signal station used in a chain of beacons linking these two places with Dinas Powys near Cardiff on the other side of the channel. This was not considered very romantic and various other reasons for its existence have been suggested; one fanciful idea was that it had been artificially created, moulded into shape by the people of Atlantis.

At one time this bit of countryside belonged to Glastonbury Abbey. The story behind how it came to be endowed to the abbey is a stirring tale of giants and giant-slayer and a strong link with King Arthur.

This green and noble hill, once known as the Mount of Frogs, was supposedly the home of three giants of a particularly nasty disposition. The prehistoric earthworks and megaliths, which can be seen at Brent Knoll, may have been responsible for the beliefs that huge giants had once lived here.

It was one Christmas and King Arthur was holding court at Caerleon in Wales, where he knighted a young man named Ider, or Yder the son of King Nuth. A test of valour was prepared for this bold knight; when Arthur was at Glastonbury he told Ider of three giants living at The Mount of Frogs and arranged a party, which included Ider, to go and march against them. The young man was over-zealous however and galloped on ahead.

He slew all three singlehanded but paid for his heroic deed with his life. Arthur was full of guilt when he returned sadly to Glastonbury. He appointed some monks to pray for Ider's soul and gave the lands around Brent Knoll to the Abbey.

This story does not completely ring true however, as Sir Ider appears in other tales of the knights of the Round Table – so perhaps King Arthur acted a little hastily!

Brent Knoll is a stirring place, an awesome mound rising up silently from the coastal plain. It is a place where, if you stand on its summit, you can see all the high spots of Somerset and many more besides. Looking out into the Bristol Channel you can see the tiny islands of Flat Holm and Steep Holm, and beyond them the faint coastline of Wales. There is a feeling of great antiquity about this place. Perhaps those giants were not so unreal after all.

REFERENCES TO Arthur abound all around Somerset. Castle Lane, says this modern road sign, leads to Camelot Fort.

THE THREE fearsome giants were slewn by the brave young knight Sir Ider on the Mount of Frogs or Brent Knoll.

DUNSTER

DUNSTER AT the gate of Exmoor is a fine example of a medieval village. During the Middle Ages it was a thriving seaport. The sea has now receded, leaving this charming little town well away from the coast.

The first view of Dunster is dominated by the magnificent castle perched high on a tor, standing guard over the cluster of houses below. The main street is wide, lined with Tudor buildings but the most striking feature is the curious octagonal shaped Yarn Market. The roof is pyramid-like with two gables on each section, the whole being supported by a central stone pillar. This building is a legacy of the cloth trade, once of great importance to the town; in fact the cloth manufactured in the area was known as 'Dunsters'.

Dunster Castle is a real fairy tale castle, the sort that could have come directly from Arthurian legends, with its medieval towers and battlements. Little wonder then there is a strong link between Dunster and King Arthur.

The Dunster story can be found in the 'life' of Carannog. The Welsh legends about the lives of the Saints quite often have reference to Arthur, as in Caradoc's *Life of Gildas* which told of the abduction of Guinevere to Glastonbury. The legend tells us Carannog had a portable altar with strange properties – among others, it floated. He launched it into the Bristol Channel and drifted, intending to preach wherever it washed ashore. It ran aground on the Somerset coast near Dunster. At this time Arthur was living at the castle with Cadwy who ruled there. When Carannog arrived in search of his altar, he encountered Arthur who refused to tell him

WITH ITS turrets, towers and battlements, Dunster Castle comes straight from the pages of a child's fairy-tale book.

its whereabouts until he proved his holiness by ridding the district of a gigantic serpent. Carannog prayed and the serpent was duly turned into a docile creature cowering at the feet of the Saint. He did not kill it however but banished it from the place for ever. Arthur dutifully returned the altar; he had tried to use it as a table but it mysteriously tossed everything to the floor. So he may have been glad to see it go!

He made Carannog a gift – a piece of land on which to build a church; this was a place called Carrum, now Carhampton near Blue Anchor. The Chapel of St Carannog stood here until the sixteenth century. Today the site lies beneath the garden of the former vicarage to the east of the present church of St John the Baptist. This may have been a romantic tale, explaining how this piece of land became church property. But it again shows us how important is the presence of Arthur in Somerset – and the writings of the Welsh monks often confirm local beliefs that King Arthur did indeed live and fight in this area.

ARTHUR'S GRAVE

'Yet somemen say in many parts of England that King Arthur is not dead, but has by the will of our Lord Jesu into another place; and men say that he shall come again and he shall win the Holy Cross ... And many men say that there is written upon the tomb this ... Hic jacet Arthurus, Rex quondam Rexque futurus'

Malory

HERE LIES the once and future king. Folklore suggests that Arthur, if he is not resting at Avalon, is sleeping in a cave, possibly beneath the Tor or under Cadbury Hill, both places have such legends relating to them. To end all the speculation the monks of Glastonbury Abbey announced in 1191 that they had unearthed the bones of King Arthur and his Queen Guinevere. How the discovery actually came about had an air of mystery to it. A Welsh bard divulged to Henry II the burial place of Arthur which up till then had been a closely guarded secret. He told the Abbot of Glastonbury the King was buried in the graveyard of the abbey south of the Lady Chapel, at great depth, between two pillars – the two stone pyramids predicted by legend. It was not until some years later that the Abbot, prompted by other hints from different sources, actually excavated the spot.

The monks dug down seven feet before reaching a stone slab, below this was a lead cross, bearing the Latin words *'Hic Jacet Sepultus Inclitus Rex Arthurius In Insula Avalonia'*. The monks dug on a further nine feet and found a coffin, a hollowed-out oak tree-trunk containing the bones of what appeared to be an immensely tall man. He appeared to have ten wounds, all healed except one. Buried in the same coffin were the remains of a smaller person, explained away as being those of Guinevere.

On April 19 1278 the bodies were removed in the presence of King Edward I and Queen Eleanor. They were placed in a black marble tomb before the high altar of the main Abbey church, and there they remained until the dissolution in 1539 when the shrine was vandalised. The spot is marked today by a board and a kerb surrounding an area of grass.

The question the historians asked and continue to ask is: 'Where was the proof?' It seemed that the whole affair may have been an ingenious twelfth century publicity stunt. After all the Abbey had in 1184 been devastated by fire and the monks were desperate for funds to rebuild it. Henry II might have been eager to disprove theories that Arthur was still alive and about to return as some kind of Messiah. This way he finally laid Arthur's ghost to rest. The iron cross that was unearthed mysteriously disappeared in the seventeenth century and the site of the grave had been rifled and vandalised during the Dissolution when the abbey itself was stripped and the walls left to crumble with neglect.

It was not until 1963 that C.A. Ralegh Radford excavated the site and confirmed there were traces of the monks' digging so many years before. Thus the supposition the monks had tried to defraud the public centuries ago was dispelled. There was a grave; it might have been Arthur and Guinevere's. The identification is still a little uncertain but Malory writes in *Morte D'Arthur* that the three ladies brought Arthur to his grave in Avalon. Sir Bedivere followed and came upon a chapel where he found a hermit grovelling by a new grave. Asking the hermit who was buried there the hermit replied he was unsure but during the night a number of ladies had carried the body to this place and implored him to inter it. *'Alas,'* said Sir Bedivere, *'that was my lord King Arthur, that here lieth buried in this chapel!'*

THE GRAVE of King Arthur and his Queen? Or a twelfth-century trick thought up by ingenious monks?

THE LEGEND
AND THE REALITY

WAS KING Arthur 'real'? Did he exist as a true King? Was he a Celtic hero, ruler and conqueror or the romantic medieval knight in shining armour?

So many theories have been suggested, so much written about him over the centuries that even though the truth may have become somewhat distorted, it is hard to believe such a person couldn't have existed to spawn all these glorious tales. There must have been a warrior worthy of the title 'King' Arthur. In early Welsh poetry there is reference to a man – or men – with the name Arthur who undertook heroic deeds and had all kinds of adventures. Folklore and history touch just occasionally to produce those romantic stories which we read as children and are still enjoyed by children today. Having read a lot of books about Arthur I can understand how legend and reality can and do become interwoven, Wives' tales and folklore always have a grain of truth somewhere and Arthur's story is no different.

Arthur appears to have been uprooted from his original era in the 5th century and literally updated; from Dark Ages to Medieval times. There is no space in history for this glorious 'King' of the Middle Ages, but he has become a romantic, legendary figure, fighter of the devil, worshipped by fair maidens and surrounded by the chivalrous knights of his round table, enthroned with his queen in Camelot.

To try to unravel the mystery surrounding him it helps to visit some of the places which lay claim to this 'Once and Future King'. The West Country has these very strong links with Arthur.

LANGPORT CHURCH in Somerset, thought to be the site of an Arthurian battle.

Cornwall and Somerset in particular, are littered with evidence of the existence of some such person. King Arthur has given his name to many sites in Wales, the North of England and Scotland but Tintagel Castle in north Cornwall is strongly believed to be his birthplace and Glastonbury Abbey, Somerset claims to be the site of his grave.

No amount of reading about Arthur will prepare you for the wonderful, breath-taking scenery that will greet you on Tintagel Head, or the serene architecture of all that remains of the abbey at Glastonbury. Whether you believe in King Arthur or not, you can still experience some of the Westcountry's most dramatic landscapes. Journeying through the locations in this book, perhaps you will ponder whether Arthur really did pass this way. One thing is certain though, and that is how much this 'legendary' figure has influenced the area. Arthur's Bridge here, Arthur's Well there: everywhere traces of the legend, showing just how important Arthur is to the Westcountry.

The small Cornish village of Tintagel has thrived on the influx of visitors in search of Arthur. He has added almost a kind of novelty to the area, but authors and poets for centuries have written about the Arthurian connection with this exceptional piece of Cornish coast. Ignore the more obvious tourist attractions and imagine Tintagel several hundred years ago, you will soon find yourself carried along by the romantic imagery of Malory's *'Morte d'Arthur'* and Tennyson's *Idylls of the King'*, fired by the historic 'biography' of King Arthur written by Geoffrey of Monmouth in the twelfth century. I have taken Tintagel as just one example of how Arthur has affected a community. Looking around at the multitude of other Arthurian sites they are all equally significant, all similarly affected by the quest for the truth about Arthur.

Geoffrey of Monmouth had a lot to answer for with his misleading *History of the Kings of Britain,* there may well have been truth in his writings but we know that he 'invented' Merlin and he 'played about' with dates, casting shadows of doubt on the whole authenticity of Arthur. On the whole the work was not considered factually very reliable. In the words of fellow Bossiney author Colin Wilson in *King Arthur Country,* Geoffrey of Monmouth's book *'contains about as much history as, say, the Irish Fairy Tales of W.B. Yeats.'*

Nevertheless he gave us a tremendous storyline and history has shown that a great warrior named Arthur did exist. The memory of our fifth/sixth century hero remains strong in so many corners of the British Isles.

THE THORN, THE GRAIL AND THE CHALICE WELL

... 'From our old books I know
Joseph came of old to Glastonbury,
And there the heathen Prince Arvigus,
Gave him an isle of Marsh whereupon to build;
And there he built with wattles from the marsh
A little lonely church in days of yore ...'
Tennyson – The Holy Grail

PERHAPS ONE of the most familiar legends known of Joseph of Arimathea and Glastonbury is the one about the Holy Thorn. Joseph is credited with bringing Christianity to the British Isles and founding the first Christian church. It is believed he founded the old church on the present site of the Abbey at Glastonbury. Traditionally he was a tin trader and may well have visited Cornwall for tin and the Mendip Hills of Somerset for lead.

On his visit to Glastonbury, Joseph and his companions arrived by boat disembarking at Wearyall Hill, here it is said that he plunged his staff into the earth where it miraculously took root. The tree that grew out of the staff became known as the Glastonbury Thorn and flowers at Christmas. The legend of the thorn is a fairly recent one but the tree itself was no figment of the imagination, it featured in the late Middle Ages, and was viewed with great reverence, it has made Glastonbury a focus for pilgrims in search of an answer to some of life's mysteries.

The original tree was cut down, after several futile attempts, but left many descendants which have been planted in various locations. A new tree was planted on Wearyall Hill in 1951 on the reputed site of Joseph's landing which had previously been marked by a stone slab.

A charming custom which has carried on for years is the sending of a spray of blossom, traditionally cut from the tree at St John's parish church in the High Street, to the Queen to decorate her table on Christmas Day. The thorn in St John's churchyard had to be cut down in 1992 but was replaced at a different site at the church. Glastonbury is a town of enigmatic quality, the flowering of this holy tree is surely symbolic of the metaphysical power of the place.

What then could be the significance of Joseph of Arimathea in connection with King Arthur? When Joseph came to Glastonbury he was supposed to have brought with him the Holy Grail, the cup which Jesus used for the sacrament at the Last Supper. The quest for the Grail is synonomous with the Arthurian legends, the knights of the Round Table undertook the task of searching for this most holy of relics. Joseph and his companions settled at Glastonbury and founded the Church which stood on the site of the abbey until it was destroyed by fire in 1184. The church was a rough affair, built of wattle, nothing like the magnificent structure which succeeded it. It was at this site that the grave of King Arthur was unearthed. If all the legends and stories are to be believed then Arthur and his knights lived almost on top of the Grail without realising it. There are enthusiasts who believe that the cup is buried beneath the well which has come to be known as Chalice Well.

In the valley between Chalice Hill and the Tor lies a peaceful secluded garden and here there is a spring, enclosed in stonework. The water which flows from this spring has never failed even in the worst drought. The speculation about the Grail being buried here is due to the properties of this water. Because of its iron content, the water which is actually crystal clear, turns the stone over which it flows a distinctive orange-red colour. This is known as the Blood Spring, people believing the chalice of Christ to be the

THE CHALICE WELL, in a peaceful garden, attracts those who seek calm and tranquillity.

cause of the 'blood-stained' water, buried in the depths below. In 1582 a Dr John Dee claimed the water had healing properties but it was not until the mid-eighteenth century that it became fashionable to 'take the water' at Glastonbury's spring. A Matthew Chancellor in 1750 dreamt that if he drank the water on seven consecutive Sundays he would be cured of his asthma. He did and he was cured. After this there was a great influx of visitors all wanting to take the 'cure', a pump house was built in Magdalene Street and the Bath House became very popular.

The excitement finally blew over but people still come to Glastonbury to take advantage of the unique beneficial qualities of the water. The garden in which the well is situated is a wonderful tranquil place reflecting the peaceful unhurried pace of the flowing waters; a spot to sit and meditate. Even here is a reference to King Arthur; the water emerges at the top of a waterfall cascading into an area known as King Arthur's Court.

From here it flows into what once was the Pilgrim's Bath where it is said many people were miraculously healed. After travelling underground again it comes out into the two symbolic circular pools. The design of these pools is reflected in the well-head cover, a wrought iron lid given in thanks for peace by Friends of Glastonbury in 1919. The design, by Frederick Bligh Bond, has links with early Christian beliefs, it has been connected with the Sacred Geometry of Glastonbury Abbey. The interlocking circles can also be translated as the Yin and the Yang, the passive and the active, the two pools directly reflect this, one being calm and the other turbulent. Altogether this makes for a place of great thoughtfulness. There is much to dwell on and the beauty of the gardens, the domain of the Chalice Well Trust, are a joy amidst the hustle and bustle of every day life.

SOMERSET REFLECTIONS

THERE IS a great deal of evidence to show Arthur travelled widely throughout the South West. Following in his footsteps takes us on a marvellous tour. In fact we could be influenced as much as Tennyson was, when he went on his Cornish and Welsh tours prior to writing *The Idylls of the King*, one of the finest works about our hero.

Arthurian legends are tales of romance and majesty woven with all the glory and trappings of the Medieval. But as we now know he lived – if he existed at all – in the fifth or sixth century: never in the Middle Ages. It was not such a glamorous time, fighting the invading Saxons, no shining armour to protect him but a leather jerkin, a gold helmet and a circular shield adorned with the likeness of the Virgin Mary. He carried with him Excalibur, the enchanted sword forged in Avalon.

Each place we have featured in this book tells a chapter in Arthur's life, from his very birth to his death, or at least his resting place from whence he will come again, the Celtic Messiah to save his country. Of all the places I have visited I think Glastonbury has left the deepest impression. It is a town full of mystery, full of hope and expectation, a town with hidden energy, the spirit of Arthur seems to linger. It is as if a complex web has been woven around it. We are lured here as the spider lures the fly … in search of the enigma of Arthur.

THE ROUND TABLE

A T A RISK of contradicting myself my journey around the Arthurian sites leads me to Winchester. Malory identifies this once capital of Wessex as Camelot, the court of King Arthur. To back this up, hanging in the Great Hall of Winchester Castle is the 'Round Table'. If you are searching for a romantic medieval setting for Arthur's Court then Cadbury hillfort in Somerset, the much fancied site cannot be it. It is lonely and isolated, a good defensible stronghold but not the bustling place of the Arthurian legends. Winchester however was at one time, before the rise of London as our capital city, a place of some importance.

The Round Table, minus its twelve legs which, sadly, have been lost, was made in either the thirteenth or fourteenth century. It was possibly used for the purpose of celebrating the then popular Arthurian festivals in which noblemen indulged. It is eighteen feet across, divided into twenty four segments (it must have been somewhat overcrowded) plus one larger space for the king. The painting on the table-top, added in 1522 by order of Henry VIII for a visit from Charles V, shows the names of Arthur's knights and depicts King Arthur, actually modelled by a very youthful Henry VIII, seated in full royal regalia. In the very centre is a Tudor rose. The idea behind the round table, of course, was that none should feel more privileged than another; it is also thought to be symbolic of the Zodiac. In some stories it is said that Merlin made the table for Uther Pendragon, Arthur's father. On his death Merlin gave the table to Arthur and his Knights thus instigating the birth of the legendary Knights of the Round Table.

There are several other 'Round Tables' to be discovered in the British Isles. Some are just mounds of earth, ancient earthworks as at Stirling Castle in Scotland and at Caerleon, Gwent. Others claim to have the 'real' thing, The Halls of Chivalry in Tintagel, Cornwall and, of course, Winchester. There is no doubt however these wooden versions did not exist in the fifth and sixth centuries in the time of King Arthur.

MERLIN CREATED the Round Table which became the mystical symbol of Arthur and his fellow knights.

FELICITY YOUNG and Michael Williams, standing by the beautiful reproduction of Arthur's round table in King Arthur's Halls in Cornwall, look up at some of the magnificent stained glass windows.
The idea of a table where all were equal, where no man sat in state above his peers appealed to the romantic idealism which, especially in Victorian times, surrounded the knightly legend. In fact, any leader of the time would have had to impose a fierce discipline – or quickly have been deposed.

STONEHENGE

STONEHENGE IS more than the great Wiltshire puzzle. Stonehenge is one of the greatest mysteries in the whole of the British Isles.

These sixteen standing and various scattered stones also have their place on our Arthurian tour of the West. As we come to the end of this, the twentieth century, they remain collectively an impressive monument. But in the old days when Salisbury Plain was open and wild, a lonely barren landscape, Stonehenge must have been even more dramatic.

Wiltshire has been called 'the cradle of our civilisation'. Arthur Mee, writing his guide to Wiltshire, back in 1929, part of his *King's England* series had this to say: '*It is the way we go back into the dim mists of time. Far off a solitary trumpet blew as Arthur rode into the night leaving Guinevere with her breaking heart at Amesbury, and it seems to us, as we walk about these ancient trackways of our race, that still far off a solitary trumpet blows.*'

In the olden times superstitious Wiltshire men and women tended to steer clear of Stonehenge. There they felt a menacing loneliness; there they felt uneasy. Some said the Devil himself had built Stonehenge.

The place is, in fact, a double mystery. Colin Wilson has said Stonehenge was a healing centre. Some say it was a temple. Others a form of entrance to the 'underworld'. Was it a means of calculating the movements of the moon and the sun? Stonehenge throws up various questions but, at heart, it remains an enigma.

How did these stones get here?

AN OLD postcard of Stonehenge.

Some of these huge stones almost certainly come from Wales. It would have been a transportation job of considerable complexity; so much so there is a theory Merlin used his magical powers to get them here! The one serious flaw in this explanation is Stonehenge was built more than two thousand years ahead of Arthur's birth.

Although Stonehenge is pre-Celtic, the character of Merlin is that of the Celtic druids, the seers. It is a reasonable assumption that Geoffrey of Monmouth and other medieval scribes drew inspiration from the folk memories of those Celtic priests.

If Arthur symbolised the military strength in the final struggle of Celtic Britain, Merlin certainly represented the magical powers.

But whether Merlin had a magical hand here is just another missing piece in the jigsaw puzzle that is Stonehenge.

Tintagel, pictured by Felicity Young and, opposite, photographed by cricketer David Halfyard in the early 1970s.

ARTHUR LIVES ON ...

ARTHUR'S reputation is legendary, like Sir Francis Drake at sea and more recently Field Marshal Viscount Montgomery on the battlefield.

Arthur, of course, was a significant character in battle. His victories were real enough, but in those distant days when written records were scarce, his fame spread through word of mouth, and doubtless each victory grew in the telling and the retelling.

And, of course, the mystery and the romance deepened in that there is no known Arthur grave. His commanders possibly rea-

*ARTHUR'S GRAVE according to some Cornish folklore. It stands along-
side the River Camel just outside Camelford.*

soned, by burying his bones in an unmarked grave they saved them from future desecration by the Saxons.

In a curious way, Arthur grew in death. Colin Wilson in his final section in *King Arthur Country*, first published by Bossiney in 1979, concluded '... *although the new Angle-land had forgotten Arthur, the Celtic bards remembered him. The legends and poems proliferated. And Arthur's real conquest – the conquest of the European imagination – began.*'

We believe the conquest will continue. The Arthurian stories have been adapted to different ages, different forms: books, novels serious volumes of history. There have been poems and plays. Arthur continues to ride across screens, large and small, galloping through our imagination, stirring speculation.

Arthur lives on – proving legend can triumph over fact.

Arthur's impact had been so powerful that for years and years after his death there was widespread belief he had *not* died. Some people even believed he would, one day, reappear and drive out the foes of Britain.

We have a hunch *something* of that lingers today.

MORE BOSSINEY BOOKS...

ABOUT EXMOOR
by Polly Lloyd

'It is a cameo to be treasured,' says Polly Lloyd who takes us on a reflective tour of this timeless corner of England.'
Book Journal

LEGENDS OF DORSET
by Polly Lloyd

The author explores legendary Dorset, visiting places as diverse as the Sacred Circle at Knowlton and Chesil Beach. Dorset is a mine of myth and folklore.

'Weird happenings...' Polly Lloyd delves through tales ranging from moving rocks to murders.
Ed Perkins, Southern Evening Echo

CURIOSITIES OF EXMOOR
by Felicity Young

'...a tour in words and pictures of the National Park embracing Somerset and Devon.'
Nancy Hammonds, Evening Herald

'Felicity Young, an artist who has contributed many drawings to Bossiney Books, makes her debut as an author with a beautiful description of Exmoor and its many delights.'
June Glover, South Hams Group of Newspapers

LEGENDS OF SOMERSET
by Sally Jones – 65 photographs and drawings

Sally Jones travels across rich legendary landscapes. Words, drawings and photographs all combine to evoke a spirit of adventure.

'On the misty lands of the Somerset plain – as Sally Jones makes clear – history, legend and fantasy are inextricably mixed.'
Dan Lees, The Western Daily Press

SUPERNATURAL IN SOMERSET
by Rosemary Clinch

Atmospheres, healing, dowsing, fork-bending and strange encounters are only some of the subjects featured inside these pages. A book, destined to entertain and enlighten – one which will trigger discussion – certain to be applauded and attacked.

'...an illustrated study of strange encounters and extraordinary powers...'
Somerset County Gazette

We shall be pleased to send you our catalogue giving full details of our growing list of titles for Devon, Cornwall, Dorset, Somerset and Wiltshire and forthcoming publications. If you have difficulty in obtaining our titles, write direct to Bossiney Books, Land's End, St Teath, Bodmin, Cornwall.